As I turned through the pages of Rashani Rea's mystical collages and Chelan Harkin's seer-like poetry, I sensed angels tapping my soul with a numinous sensation. Their combined artistry touches the spot where our soul seeks to express our infinite genius. I felt like I was walking inside a stream, sensing how life is held, seen, and heard. How the ordinary is extraordinary when we take time to pray with Nature, listen to our insights, and follow our hearts. Each piece is a full sound and a meditation. When we allow our rawness and our vulnerabilities to kiss the lips of our trueness.

–**Carolyn Riker**, poet & author, author of *This is Love* and *Blue Clouds*

In the same way as a bird has to open its wings in order to fly, we have to open our hearts so as to truly live. This is the message underpinning this stunningly beautiful book *Taste the Sky*. Rashani Rea's soulful artwork combined with the sublime poetry of Chelan Harkin make each page an experience to savour and deeply reflect upon. Just like the ancient contemplative practice of Lectio Divina, there is a hidden music on each and every page, that cries out to be listened to from the "ear of our heart." Allow this beautiful book to draw you deeper into the mysterious depths of your being; that place where our individual wholeness and the transcendence of our individual wholeness meet. I shall treasure this book, and read it again and again, for it is such a wonderful joy.

–**Christopher Goodchild**, author of *Unclouded by Longing* and *The Winds of Homecoming*

This book is a coalescence of Soul-inspired art with Soul-inspired words. It is a natural union of the heart with the mind, the mind with the heart. Together they become one. Each collage created for each chosen phrase is a meditation in and of itself. It is a book to be savored slowly, with enough time to be absorbed again and again.

–**Shiana Seitz**, author of *Morning Words* and *First You Let it Go*

I have found in these current times, it is the little treasures of truths that capture your mind, spark your spirit, and stir a resonance of your soul by tiny powerful snippets. This can be for us a fundamental, encouraging, daily dose of medicine that we can actualize, absorb and elevate. *Taste the Sky* is just that. Rashani Réa's collages come from a depth of a life lived in art, nature, mindful community and supporting others through the underworlds of loss and grief. Both Rashani and Chelan have surrendered to the mystic within, becoming conduits of reciprocity with the muse of the outer mystic— that speaks through us in some divine presence. The first time I came across Chelan Harkin's words I was taken, and that love affair of prose hasn't stopped, it just keeps deepening. The two paired is a little heaven upon your bedside or coffee table. A tangible portal into the mystery.

–**K.M. McCauley Anast**, author of *Myrtle, Shifting Shadows Through Grief & Cancer* and *Befriending an Unlikely Ally*

Rashani's inspiring collage art and Chelan's ageless wisdom merge perfectly in this carefully crafted and congruent book. The world needs more of this kind of beauty. Thank you, both, for this generous offering.

–**David Tensen**, founder of Poetry Chapel™, author of *The Wrestle*

Open this co-creation of radiance, and you'll find a sea of wonder, latitudes of joy, smoldering longings, kidney wisdom, big-hearted prayers, rebel-mystic essence, and the marrow of the Divine Feminine. On every page a discovery, on every page the awe of awakening. *Taste the Sky* is a collection of collages, but more: glowing, flowing, wild, and awake, the images are the transfigured raiment of verse; and the reflecting poetry, is cool water come deep red wine. Taken together — the fragrant distillate of love. And all of it, under the constant eye of wonder, arrives laden with promise. Love made visible in the weaving. And there are no doilies here. The collages are like stalwart sojourners: mystics and musicians, doulas and dark mead brewers. And dancers, definitely dancers. In a world parched by brute politics, scorched by rancour and war, pause, sink into these collages, taste and see, there are yet wings for humanity.

–**Stephen Berg,** author of *Beacons, Blues and Holy Goats*

Rashani Réa's collage art and Chelan Harkin's poetry are a heavenly match made by two women who are clearly aligned with source energy. Each page of this beautiful, soulful, necessary book quiets the noise, fills me with breath, and draws me closer to what is real and true and holy inside of me, inside each of us, inside the world. This will be one of those books to return to again and again.

–**Julia Fehrenbacher,** author of *Staying in Love*

What gorgeous love alchemy this book!
so endlessly revealing.
Rashani distills music to color with indigenous base tones and finely pearled silence.
Chelan's gorgeous wakeful poetry, summoned from the same source,
—wild yet simple—dances and sings direct to our heart.
This union of color, texture and song comes home to us intense, transparent, still breathing.

–**Velusia Van Horssen,** essential and contemplative poet

The way Rashani has of weaving together words and images touches a part of me that is singing the same song, crying with the longing to be One, to be known, to be felt. And Chelan Harkin's poetry opens a place in me that cracks open my heart, and helps my Soul take flight…to the place I know we all belong…. far beyond this world and yet intimately one with everything. Thank you Rashani and Chelan for sharing such beauty with the world.

–**Rajyo Allen,** co-founder of Samasati Sanctuary, author of *Fumbling Towards Freedom: Initiations on the Journey Home to Myself*

Like a portal opening into another world, Réa's art in this book is powerful and primal, capturing the eye with a unique sense of design and a boundless imagination. Light seems to be ever-present as deep colours interweave effortlessly, crystallizing in thirty-eight striking images the essence of the divine. Juxtaposed with Harkin's illuminating words, this is a book that truly does make love visible, revealing the sensitivity and passion of a writer and artist both creating in unison at the top of their game. An expression of spiritual vision that revels in a different perspective and the full scope of the mystic, this is a book that all lovers of heart-truth will treasure for many years.

–**C.W. Blackburn,** poet – *Where Words Are Yet to Be Spoken: Poems for Presence*

The book *Taste the Sky* is the exquisite result of the collaboration between two mystic artists—the collage artist Rashani Réa and the poet Chelan Harkin. One could imagine that Rashani Réa depicts with her inspirational collages vast cosmic energies and at the same time we can find these forces also in our own sacred heart. Her unique art invites us into inner stillness and being centred. Peace exudes from every one of her collages and calls us to be Here Now. Chelan Harkin describes in her poetry the process of inner healing—which is personal as well as universal. She calls us to open our heart to love and to embrace our shadows in naked honesty. Her invitation to compassion for ourselves leads to compassion and understanding for others. Chelan Harkin brings thru her poetry the Divine to earth right into our humanness—close to our heart—where it belongs—the only place we can truly find it.

—**Mirjam Temba Rothkamm**, artist, author, poet, meditation teacher in Australia

Behold! Witness in both courageous action and form these glimpses of a future unfolding through this beautiful book. Immanence and transcendence coalescing into vehicles of light. Originality awakened in two whole human beings coming together in an expression of a joyful connection to life! I see that such co-creative collaboration is a natural yet miraculous goodness, a revelation of our inherent human capacity to inspire each other's lives, uplifting us into the mysterious, the unexpected, the endlessly new. Filled with a direct experience of love and obvious devotion; an action arising in being itself. Thank you both as we humans need clear examples of a hidden destiny for us all as each of our true voices finds all their diverse ways into being…gracefully we are drawn together with results that none of us could do alone. Thank you for this direct inspiration and experience of the heart's genius in action.

—**Carol W. Stewart**, founder of "The Mystery School," an endless work in progress devoted to deepening the articulation of the Tarot, the Medicine Wheel and The Tree of Life.

Taste the Sky by artist Rashani Réa and poet Chelan Harkin is a delicate movement of art and words that draws the soul into a place of serene consciousness. Thought provoking and creating a beautiful belonging into the balance of these two creative ways, I find that this book holds a sacredness of its own. The breathtaking creativity captivates you and touches the longing of your heart. The beauty of it woven so deeply into the spiraling of our lives. What is created here is a wonderment, a stirring of being deep within one's seeking. Words and art that fold tenderly over you, through you, and with you. *Taste the Sky* is a book to hold close to your heart. Let it touch your daily journey, your pathway in a deep and meaningful way.

—**Maureen Kwiat Meshenberg**, author and poet, sacred writing circle facilitator

Taste the Sky has a polychoral effect of multi-sensory tonality and visual form. Rashani's heartfelt pairing with Chelan's inner sight transmit the mystic's teaching ~ with a foot in each world; form and formless, inner and outer, bridging dimensions, coming undone, within a vast sky interfacing two worlds ~ shimmering, shaking, resolving and evolving. This book is a medicinal balm for the soul and shows a pathway for those who dare to wander off the beaten path!

—**Kim Lincoln,** author of *Holy Here Wholy You, Discovering Your Authentic Self* and *Soul Power, You Loving You*

Taste the Sky

Love Made Visible Through Art and Poetry

Taste the Sky

Love Made Visible Through Art and Poetry

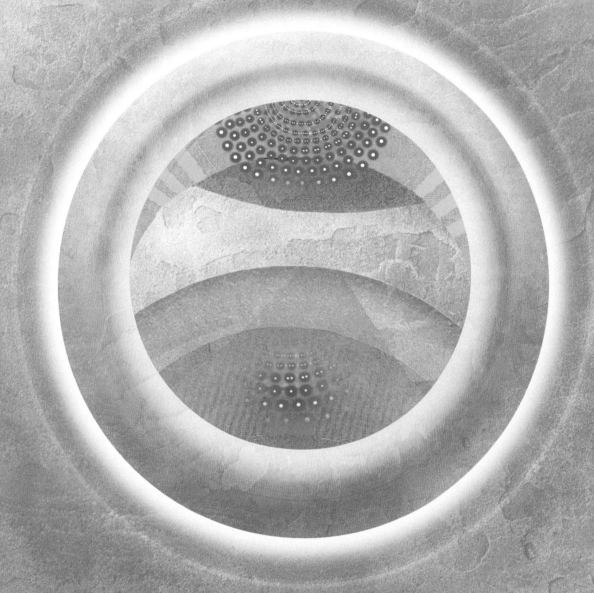

Rashani Réa & Chelan Harkin
Foreword by Aha Lisa de Jong

To order additional copies of this book, contact:
Xlibris
844-714-8691
www.Xlibris.com
Orders@Xlibris.com

ISBN: Softcover   978-1-6698-3004-7
        EBook   978-1-6698-3003-0

Print information available on the last page

Rev. date: 06/29/2022

Until i see that i am nothing,
i cannot see that i am
Everything

–Marguerite Porete

(A French mystic, condemned as a heretic and burned at the stake in 1310.)

To our mothers, Christina Thomsen Harris and Irene Knight Weiler, and to the countless women mystics—known and unknown—who have blessed this planet with their primordial grace and timeless wisdom. I'm sure there are many more of you whose names I have never heard of, some who are alive today and many others who walked the earth—barefoot and bare-breasted—who existed long before the concept of "clockocracy" replaced the Dreamtime, before the Gregorian calendar eliminated the natural cycles of the sun and the ancient rhythms of the moon; long before churches and synagogues and man-made temples were created; centuries before the annexation of the world took place—prior to the concoction of all religions, when earth-based spirituality was celebrated and revered. This book is dedicated to each and *all* of you. And though I don't know your names, you live vibrantly inside of me.

In deep, unspeakable gratitude I bow and sing joyously to those of you whose names I do know:

'Ahotk, Natalie Diaz, A'isha al-Ba'uniyya, Aisha Al-Manoubya, Albruna, Alexandra David-Néel, Alice Bailey, Alice Walker, Akka Mahadevi, Amanda Gorman, Amma Sri Karunamayi, Ana Lisa de Jong, Anandamayi Ma, Angela of Foligno, Anna Kingsford, Anne Catherine Emmerich, Annette Kaiser, Annie Besant, Ásíyih Khánum, Bahíyyih Khánum, Beatrice of Nazareth, Bebe Nanaki, Britt Posmer, Bodhmall, Bridget of Sweden, Carol Stewart, Catherine of Siena, Catherine Tekakwitha, Cemalnur Sargut, Christina Harris, Christina of Markyate, Clarissa Pinkola Estés, Consolata Betrone, Daya Mata, Dhyani Ywahoo, Dorothy Walters, Dove White, Edna St. Vincent Millay, Edith Stein, Eleonora Duse, Elizabeth of the Trinity, Elizabeth Reninger, Elizabeth Updike, Emily Dickinson, Etty Hillesum, Fannie Lou Hamer, Florence Scovel Shinn, Flower A. Newhouse, Gangasati, Gargi Vachaknavi, Gemma Galgani, Gertrude the Great, Ghosha, Gitta Mallasz, Gurumayi Chidvilasananda, Hadewijch, Hannah Rachel Verbermacher, Harriet Tubman, Hatshepsut, Hazrat Babajan, Heilwige Bloemardinne, Helena Blavatsky, Helena Roerich, Hilde Domin, Hildegard von Bingen, Helen Keller, Hypatia, Irena Tweedie, Isaignaniyar, Isadora Duncan, Itala Mela, Jan Frazier, Jeanne-Marie Bouvier de la Motte-Guyon, Jennifer Bonadio, Jessica Fleming, Jett Psaris, Joan of Arc, Joanna Macy, Joy Bostic, Joy Harjo, Juju of Ka'u, Julian of Norwich, Kathryn Jean Lopez, Kathryn Tarananda, Kim Rosen, Kirtana, Lalla Zaynab, Lalleshvari (aka Lalla), Leslie Marmon Silko, Leslie Sarofeen, Lilian Staveley, Linda Hogan, Lopamudra, Mabel Collins, Lyla June, Ma Devi Jnanabhanishta, Maitreyi, Maniko Dru Dadigan, Margery Kempe, Marguerite Bays, Marguerite Porete, Maria Bolognesi, Maria Domenica Lazzeri, Maria Maddalena de'Pazzi, Marie de l'Incarnation, Marie Laveau, Marie Claire Schultheis, Marthe Robin, Mary Oliver, Mary Reed, Mātā Amritānandamayī Devī (aka Amma), May Sarton, Maya Angelou, Mechthild of Magdeburg, Mirabai Starr, Miranda MacPherson, miriam louisa simons, Mother Meera, Mother Shipton, Nel Houtman, Pamela Wilson, Patacara, Pema Salem, Ptesáŋwiŋ (aka White Buffalo Woman), Queen Priestess Jezebel, Rabi'a al-Adawiyya, Rachel Naomi Renen, Ralitza Zaya Benazzo, Rebecca Cox Jackson, Rosanna Deerchild, Rose Ausländer, Samiha Ayyerdi, Sant Andal, Sant Avvaiyar, Sant Bahinabai, Sant Janabai, Sant Kanhopatra, Sant Mirabai, Sant Molla, Sant Muktabai, Sant Nirmala, Sant Rupa Bhawani, Sant Sahajo Bai, Sant Sakhubai, St. Beatrice of Silva, St. Clare of Assisi, St. Catherine of Genoa, Sarada Devi, Serinity Young, Shiana Seitz, Sister Antonia de Cristo, Sister Champa, Simone Weil, Sister Nivedita, Sitt al-'Ajam, Sojourner Truth, Sokhna Magat Diop, Sun Bu'er, Susan Moon, Táhirih, Ta'Kaiya Blaney, Teresa of Ávila, Tessa Priest, Thea Bowman, The Mother, Thérèse of Lisieux, Toni Packer, Þorbjörg Lítilvölva, Yaśodharā, Yeshe Tsogyal, Uppalavanna, Ursula de Jesus, Vimala Thakar, Violet Knight, Zenshin Florence Caplow

Foreword

Infinitely deep. In the words of Chelan Harkin—*There has always lived, here in this world, a love which is infinitely deep.*

There is a light in the centre of Rashani Rea's collages that draws me deeply in. Accompanied by Chelan Harkin's extraordinary, reassuring and powerful poetry—Rashani's latest collages in this beautiful, burgeoning gift of a book—provide a window to a wider world. The one we see when we look within.

In the words of T.S. Elliot's famous poem 'Burnt Norton' (*The Four Quartets*) there is a still point in the midst of the turning world. A centre point in time from which the dance gravitates from.

At the still point of the turning world. Neither flesh nor fleshless;
Neither from nor towards; at the still point, there the dance is,
But neither arrest nor movement. And do not call it fixity,
Where past and future are gathered. Neither movement from nor towards,
Neither ascent nor decline. Except for the point, the still point,
There would be no dance, and there is only the dance.

And there is a still point in the centre of Rashani's collages, that moves and glows, that impels and quietens, that returns to us our own steady gaze.

And in Chelan's poetry there is a depth of understanding to mirror this, framed and magnified by the beauty of Rashani's art. These two artists' creations, so beautifully aligned are made to be portrayed together. Each drawing the other out into deeper and deeper truth, clarity and beauty.

Thomas Merton, in his book *Conjectures of a Guilty Bystander,* talked about le Point Vierge, the Virgin Point, as the pure glory of God in us, expressing it as *a pure diamond, blazing with the invisible light of heaven. It is in everybody, and if we could see it we would see these billions of points of light coming together in the face and blaze of a sun that would make all the darkness and cruelty of life vanish completely.*

This virgin point or 'point of nothingness' (which is not nothingness at all) that Thomas Merton refers to, is found in different forms in many great wisdom traditions, and in my own mind is the pure point of connective truth where the world's faiths and wisdom traditions meet. It is the shared humanity of us all, and what in our own Maori culture in Aotearoa, New Zealand is called 'mauri', 'the life force' that resides in the 'wairua' (spirit) of each of us.

And Chelan's words, selected here by Rashani as inspiration to her accompanying art, seem to centre in on this God-spark in us all, the centre of ourselves mirroring the great mystery.

Indeed, *where to begin about the wonders in the dilating mystery of the heart?* –Chelan Harkin

This stunning selection of word images, echoes the eternal words of Thomas Merton: *No despair of ours can alter the reality of things; or stain the joy of the cosmic dance which is always there. Indeed, we are in the midst of it, and it is in the midst of us, for it beats in our very blood, whether we want it to or not. Yet the fact remains that we are invited to forget ourselves on purpose, cast our awful solemnity to the winds and join in the general dance.*

Not forgetting also the women mystics, artists and writers throughout the ages, of which both Chelan and Rashani can count themselves, the light shining through the collages and accompanying words in this book speak to me of the divine light perceived in the 'mauri' (life essence) threaded through all things, luminous and unbroken in its woven patterns, in its spiraling and spinning cosmic dance, its never ending momentum.

Into what pattern, into what music have the spheres whirled us,
Of travelling light upon spindles of the stars wound us,
The great winds upon the hills and in hollows swirled us.

–Kathleen Raine, from 'Into What Pattern', (*Collected Poems of Kathleen Raine*)

I, the fiery life of divine essence, am aflame beyond the beauty of the meadows, I gleam in the waters, and I burn in the sun, moon, and stars.… I awaken everything to life. The air lives by turning green and being in bloom. The waters flow as if they were alive. The sun lives in its light.…

And thus, I remain hidden in every kind of reality as a fiery power. Everything burns because of me in such a way as our breath constantly moves us, like the wind-tossed flame in a fire. All of this lives in its essence, and there is no death in it. For I am life.

–Hildegard von Bingen, (*Book of Divine Works*)

–Ana Lisa de Jong

This morning before dawn I opened my laptop to begin writing an introduction for *Taste the Sky*—the book that you are now holding. While glancing quickly through a long list of emails in the inbox, I noticed an email from Matthew Fox via The Shift Network, sent at 4:02 a.m. Though I was intending to only write before the sun appeared—and not read emails—my index finger gently tapped the bold font in the small rectangular box.

I felt summoned by the synchronicity. Matthew is a remarkable theologian and contemporary mystic who I deeply respect. His "creation spirituality" is stunning. He focuses on what he calls the "primal sacraments," which are land, wind, sea and fire, life — the universe itself. I love how unexpected gifts arrive like this.

Beneath the Shift Network logo were the following words, sent as a personalized group missive:

> "Dear Rashani,
>
> It's no secret that we are living in fraught times, dangerous times, times that are demanding — on our souls, psyches, communities, and the planet itself.
>
> How do we ground ourselves so that we can keep our balance, act out of integrity, and contribute to a saner, safer, and more sustainable world?
>
> This is where the mystics come in — including the mystics in ourselves.
>
> That is the main reason for listening to the mystics—because *they awaken the mystic in us.* Carl Jung wrote, "It is to the mystics that we owe what is best in humanity."
>
> Mystics not only name the depths of living, its joys and its tragedies, but also give us practices that allow us to stay centered and on a right path through difficult times — a path that includes celebration and gratitude on one hand, yet also silence and attention to the suffering in ourselves and the world on the other..."

As a mystic who has traversed a "pathless journey" since childhood—hurled unexpectedly from what seemed like security and stability at the age of twelve, when my 19-year-old brother was found dead one morning—I resonate with everything expressed here except the part about staying centered on "a right path". Having been introduced to and profoundly influenced by Jiddu Krishnamurti five years after my brother died, I was—and continue to be—in alignment with what he referred to as "the pathless land". In 1929, during a talk in Ommen, Holland, Krishnamurti said to a group of more than three thousand people, "I maintain that Truth is a pathless land, and you cannot approach it by any path whatsoever, by any religion, by any sect..."

Also, I find it impossible these days to label anything as right or wrong. A-n-d, at the same time, I understand completely what is being expressed in the above words. I'm all for celebration and gratitude, silence and paying attention to the suffering in ourselves and throughout the world.

Yes, I discovered during puberty that *security and stability are not the ultimate foundations,* as Chelan Harkin says in one of her poems:

> "security and stability are not the ultimate foundations
> love is
> and She is a wild, thrashing thing
> and in Her desire for all of you
> She will undo you from everything."

There are probably several definitions of the word, "mystic". The definition that rings true for me in this moment is by Mirabai Starr, author of *Wild Mercy: Living the Fierce and Tender Wisdom of the Women Mystics.* She writes, *"A mystic is a person who has a direct experience of the sacred, unmediated by conventional religious rituals or intermediaries."* For some people, the word itself might seem occult or other-worldly. We know of ancient mystics but what does it mean to be a present-day mystic and how can we locate that in ourselves? Being a mystic is not some grandiose, supernatural state of being. Present-day mystics come in all shapes and sizes, ages, genders, sexual orientations, ethnicities and nationalities, castes, colors and creeds. And like Shambhala warriors, they wear no insignias or uniforms that distinguish them from anybody else. My friend, Leslie Lembo, wrote a song with a refrain that says, *I'm just a frustrated mystic living in the modern world.*

As a teenager, I discovered that the village in southern Denmark where my maternal grandparents are from was well known for its mystics. My mother definitely carried that ancestral legacy and passed it on to her children and grandchildren.

Where Chelan Harkin and I meet is in the wondrous field, which Jalāl al-Dīn Rumi described as "beyond ideas of wrongdoing and rightdoing".

Out beyond ideas of wrongdoing and rightdoing there is a field. I'll meet you there. **—Rumi**

Thank you, Chelan, for meeting me here. It is from this expansive, nondual field of infinite potential and unbroken singularity that creativity is birthed and that the illusion of separation dissolves. We inter-are[1] in this vast ocean of being out of which all sentient beings are birthed into existence. And *at the same time*, we are ordinary, individuated earthlings dealing with life's challenges—in our imperfect, idiosyncratic, mortal ways. There's no hierarchy here.

---

1   *Interbeing* is a verb created by Thich Nhat Hanh who was my root teacher for many years. He often explained that the verb "to be" can be deceptive because it implies separation. "To be" he gently reminded us is actually to "inter-be". He believed that reality is more accurately defined by *interbeing* since everything that exists in the entire cosmos—including all sentient beings—is inextricably interconnected.

The inner mystic is the part of us all that is not so interested in achievements or accomplishments but/and is ceaselessly drawn towards and into the territory of sheer wonder—to directly experience the true nature of all that is. The mystics I know, with a few flamboyant exceptions, live simply and unpretentiously—in an uncontrived way—being as natural as can be while staying deeply rooted in and connected with what is most essential, and therefore sacred.

It's important to remember that we are *all* particles, poised to become waves—and that some of us are not so poised. Humans have a way of dividing the unified field into endless, apparently separate parts when in actual fact, reality is an unfragmentable, seamless, interconnected web pulsing with life, constantly and interdependently co-arising.

When first discovering the poetry of Chelan Harkin, two and a half years ago, it was clear to me that her words emanated from an untainted Source and came to/through her in the same way that collages come to/through me, emanating from the same Source. We are both empty reeds; conduits "being used by the field" for something greater wanting to be shared with the collective. I also realized while first reading her poems that Chelan is someone—like me—who is not afraid to fully engage with—and be broken open, humbled & tumbled and initiated by—the mundane, the messiness, the pain and discomfort of this intricate and intimate dance of life. *The vaudeville of impermanence* as Stephen Levine aptly called it!

And though we have not yet met in person, there is a profound connection simply by this alone. When we spoke for the first time, we shared how when we are seized by the muse—the Unknowable Mystery— we both experience being emptied and filled at the same time. We also discovered that as well as being mothers, and daughters of amazing women, we have both devoted our lives to this unknowable, ungraspable, ineffable process which some might call "being a servant of the Heart."

Several of the collages in this book were created in the aftermath of mass shootings, which took place last month. I still remember the shock reverberating through my body when I read the headlines, "UVALDE, Texas — At least 19 children and two teachers were killed Tuesday when a gunman opened fire in a Texas elementary school, according to the Texas Department of Public Safety."

After reading about the violent murdering of innocent children and teachers, I quietly disappeared into my studio for many hours at a time and didn't spend much time with anyone else—including my partner—for several days. The intense shock, anguish and horror that resounded through my entire being forced me to stay acutely attentive and present with my personal outrage—as well as with a greater collective lamentation and keening—and the Muse took over from there.

Joanna Macy's wise words are a great comfort: *The sorrow, grief and rage you feel is a measure of your humanity and your evolutionary maturity. As your heart breaks open there will be room for the world to heal.*

Having been a death doula and grief whisperer for more than thirty years, I now experience grief, rage and sorrow as three aspects of a natural, potent alchemical energy for transformation. When I welcome this holy trinity and fully surrender into its sacred talons—relinquishing all resistance—the sense of a separate self peacefully dissolves, in the same way it dissolves when being seized by unstoppable creativity. Suddenly "I" am nothing and everything, nobody *and* everybody, resting as awareness without needing to access thoughts. In these timeless openings, the egoic identity often disappears into "the ecological Self".

These collages interwoven with excerpts of Chelan's poetry can't bring back the beautiful children and adults who were killed—or those who may be killed in the future—but perhaps they can remind you that beauty needn't be obliterated in times of suffering; that beauty might be a homeopathic dose of peace and justice in its own indescribable, sovereign way. In the words of Terry Tempest Williams: "Beauty is not optional, it is a strategy for survival."

Intrinsic to all beings, beauty renders our experience knowable—without referencing thought. Beauty has been the antidote for many painful and challenging situations for as long as I can remember. My mother taught me about shibui—a particular aesthetic of simple, subtle, and unobtrusive beauty—and my father was a professor of aesthetics—a branch of philosophy that deals with the nature of beauty as well as the philosophy of art, so I was steeped in beauty from a very young age.

Chelan beautifully says, "Whether or not you taste the sky you are building the future of humanity's wings." I love how her words can catapult the conditioned mind out of its binary, conceptual niche into a nondual, panoramic awareness—even if only for a nanosecond! After all, it's often in the repetition of these short moments of recognition—in which we glimpse the essence of all that is—that we drop effortlessly into a natural state of relaxation and equanimity.

I experience depth as well as a delightful light-heartedness permeating the invisible fabric of Chelan Harkin's poetry. She is—consciously or unconsciously—inviting us to assume the sky-like vastness of naked awareness. Some of us will kneel and others will bow or whirl, somersault or sing, keen or cry—as we each discover our own congruent ways to *Taste the Sky*.

> May we come to understand, be released from—and eventually awakened by—
> the veils of confusion and the invisible knots of ignorance that are so prevalent in this
> world. And may our miraculous earth walk here be of benefit to all beings,

Rashani Réa
6 · 6 · 2022

Taste the Sky quite simply rocks my world. I am at once its co-creator and its honored celebrator. One of the gifts of inspiration flowing through as it has in the creation of this book is that because so much of the credit for what we've created goes to The Great, Beautiful Unknown, it feels completely aligned to fully cheer it on, with uninhibited devotional-grade vigor.

A few years ago, before I had this wild, poetic breakthrough in which the Goddess started rather unabashedly and torrentially pouring Her inspiration rivers through me, I was equal parts envier and admirer of a man named Fred LaMotte. Fred is one of my all-time favorite people and poets and often jeweled snippets of his stunning poetry would be set within these hauntingly beautiful collage pieces by an artistic wizardess, Rashani Réa, who I hadn't yet met. I sighed a fantasy to myself thinking it'd be a top of the mountain experience for my poetry to ever be paired with Rashani's dazzling, transportive artistic touch.

So, it is a profound joy and honor to now be collaborating with the one and only Rashani.

Rashani's dharma art reminds me of a potion made of melted, swirling fire opals that pours its magic into you simply by beholding it. I love it so much and my soul lets out a sacred squeal of gratitude and joy seeing our creations come together throughout these pages.

I am so touched and delighted by the particular pieces of my poems that spoke to Rashani to be included in this book.

Some of these poems sing of the wonders within life eagerly waiting to be rediscovered by your heart. Some speak of claiming the agency to redefine our relationship with things that matter most—prayer, suffering, God—that we may live lives that feel closer to ourselves and that hold more of our hearts in a wider embrace. Some of these poems strive to normalize and honor our suffering and to restore our darkness with the sacred. Some have a non-dual element to them which encourages connection with a deeper, more fine-tuned inner guidance system that lives beneath our judgments and guides us from love rather than fear.

I relish the diversity of theme and tone that is represented in this book both in Rashani's art and my poetry. Each piece in this collection will ring the gong of a different energy center in your body—*Taste the Sky* reverberates with bold beauty.

As a poet and a scientist of how to unlock the joy embedded in existence, one of my delighted, ongoing explorations is the consideration of the utility of poetry specifically and of creative expression in general. What can poetry and art *do* for *or to* a person?

For a decade I worked as a hypnotherapist. Hypnotherapy basically consists of two elements: bringing people into a connected, receptive, empowered and deeply peaceful and aware state and once there, consensually delivering to the wise, fertile ground of their subconscious mind, messages that are aligned with their beautiful intentions for their lives. When these messages are accepted and absorbed, this process activates profound change.

Similarly, art and poetry, especially when paired together as they are in this book, have just this effect—to induce a beautiful, open and receptive state in the viewer—a reverent beauty trance, if you will—and then in delivering or affirming a message that helps the reader view themselves or the world in a more wondrous light, a meaningful process of beautiful change can be catalyzed.

Furthermore, because my words and Rashani's images dance together on the same page, an automatic healing experience happens on each page of this book as simultaneously viewing images with words balances both hemispheres of our brain. When this balance happens, we feel harmonious and relaxed, we feel deeper ease and our energy channels can open and flow to carry new and inspired insights to our consciousness that the reader can then incorporate into creative expression of their own! This, in part, explains the phenomenon of creativity being contagious. One definition of effective art is that it actually creates an inspired and expressive state—relaxed, open and excited with new information—in its recipient that primes them for creating inspired art of their own and joy of joys—the flame spreads!

Another interesting similarity between hypnotherapy and mystical poetry is that they are both tools to create new and beneficial associations in the deep mind. Being intentional about the power of association is one of the most profound tools a poet can wield. My poetry strives to create new associations with God, or the ultimate authority, as being unconditionally loving, playful, sweet, bursting with joy, intimate and generous in giving permission to be more fully yourself. To even imagine these possibilities can have profound implications on a life. My poetry loves to associate sensitivity and power, or humility and power, and often juxtaposes the darkness or the wound with beauty and an element of the sacred with the hope of exonerating and integrating that which we once kept hidden away in shame.

Both poetry and art are great givers of permission. They say with their example, "express and create for the sake of beauty, life and joy. Bring your truth forward. Bring your beauty forward. It belongs in this world and it is necessary." *Taste the Sky* represents permission to open to the possibility of artistic flow that is free and inspired. It's also always fun to powerfully show up representing the creative genius that can flow through women…am I right, Rashani? What a gift to give like this.

It is a wonderful thing to collaborate with someone who has a mature, whole and inclusive relationship with the mystical, or, in other words, has tasted all that is real, wounded and beautiful within the heart and honors it all. I feel deeply safe and free in relationship with people who understand the darkness and the light to be the deepest allies or sacred servants to each other. For both the darkness and the light of my poetry to be held and honored and handled with the exquisite care of Rashani's capable heart and hands has been a superb and comforting gift.

Taste the Sky is vibrating with an aliveness that yearns to kiss you awake and drench you in your own beauty. It is a compelling and evocative force of activation ready to stir up latent energies in its readers and inspire the soul's full range of movement to hesitate less to dance.

And it will also look damn good on a coffee table.

—Chelan Harkin
6 • 15 • 2020

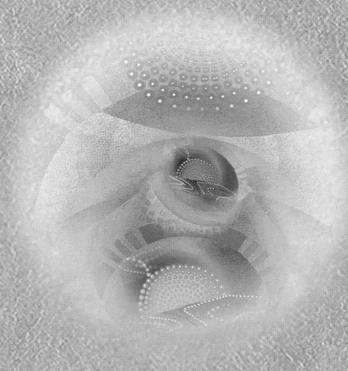

A poem is a thumbprint of the soul—
the page wants you to leave your evidence.

The world needs your voice.

Awkward truth, dull truth, messy truth, scared truth, cruel truth, hideous truth, innocent truth, sacred truth, profane truth, breathtaking truth, maddeningly plain truth, beautiful truth— the voice of your living, genuine experience.

Put me amidst life's
simplest things
that give their lives to blooming
or quietly glowing
without reaching for a name

Even when
you feel threadbare,
remember: Spectacular and
extraordinary and fully worthy
are simply part of the fabric
you and all things are
spun from

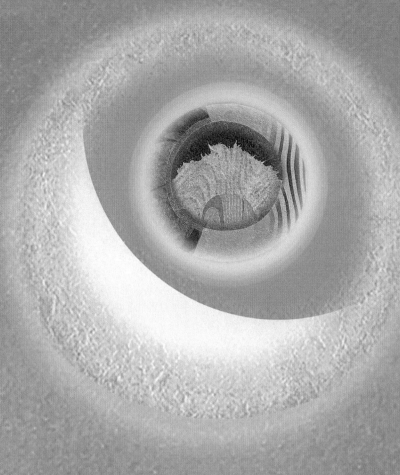

IT'S NOT SO MUCH
THAT I WANT TO WORSHIP GOD
AS FOR MY DEVOTIONAL PRACTICE
TO BE OPENING
MY BODY TO THE LIVING SCRIPTURE
OF LIFE'S MOVEMENT
AS SHE DANCES HER DESIRES
THROUGH ME
AND TO REMEMBER
TO SAY THANK YOU
WITH DEEP RECOGNITION
FOR EVERY SMALL ACT OF LOVE
THAT FINDS ME...

IT'S NOT SO MUCH
THAT I BELIEVE IN GOD
AS IT'S BEEN TAUGHT
BUT THAT ALL I DESIRE
IS TO SERVE
THE ONE GREAT HEART
THAT LIVES WITHIN
US ALL.

I don't
like the word God.
G-O-D,
God.
Two hard consonants
shut like solid doors around the 'O'
the Oh! the Awe, the softly infinite.
But creak open the hard walls around this name
as far as your hinges have learned to give
and throw the 'G' and the 'D' like twigs
into whatever you want to call
the enormity of that blaze
that feeds the 'O'
the Awe,
the
Circle

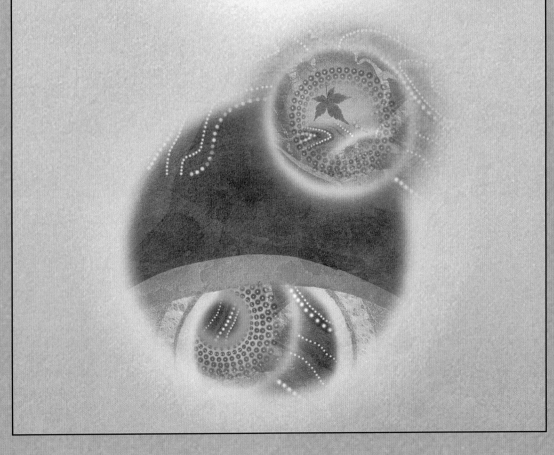

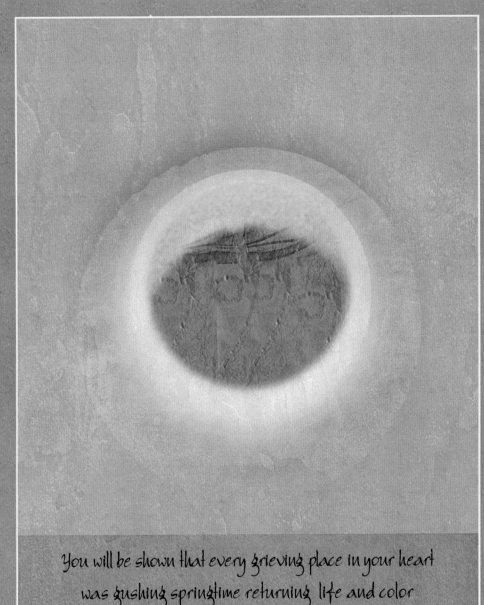

You will be shown that every grieving place in your heart
was gushing springtime returning life and color
to the world with its great willingness to feel again

There has always lived,
here in this world,
a love
that is infinitely deep.

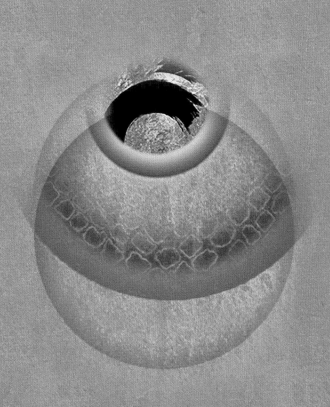

It's an unspeakable honor that so much truth
in humanity's undercurrents has swept my pen in
to write of this wild flow.

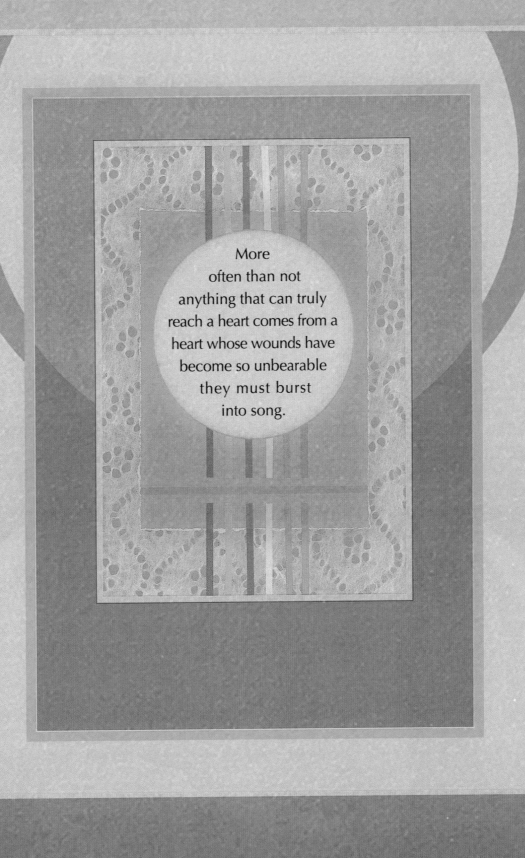

More
often than not
anything that can truly
reach a heart comes from a
heart whose wounds have
become so unbearable
they must burst
into song.

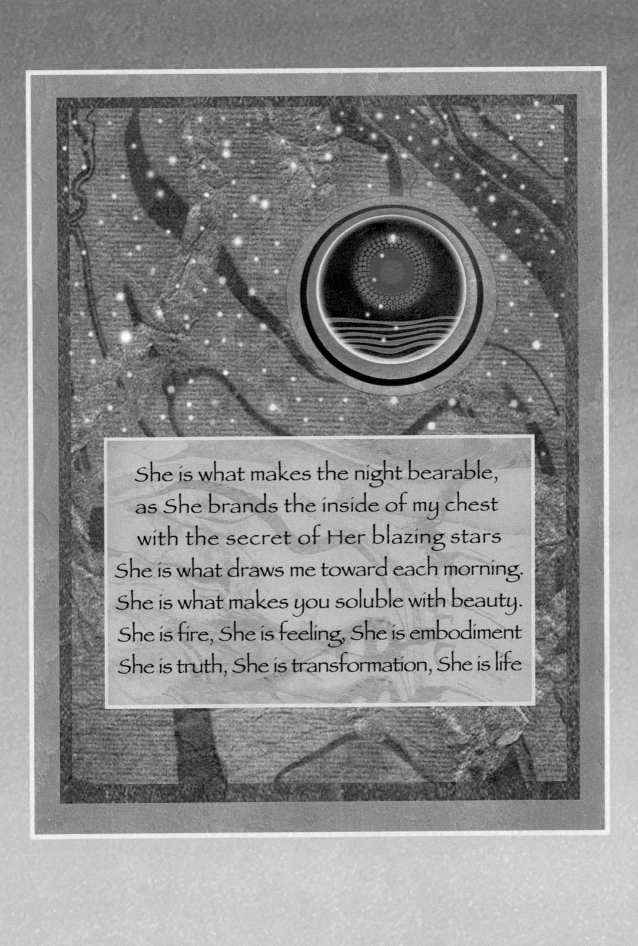

She is what makes the night bearable,
as She brands the inside of my chest
with the secret of Her blazing stars
She is what draws me toward each morning.
She is what makes you soluble with beauty.
She is fire, She is feeling, She is embodiment
She is truth, She is transformation, She is life

Drink in this special tincture of starlight.
Take in a concentrated dose of beauty
during and between meals.

Put the warm compress of sunlight
over every part of your body
and know of a certainty
there has only ever been one You!

Who would have made circles and cycles and softness
and yielding the rule ?
Who would have paused to make the exquisite flowering
of every living thing susceptible to light ?

I NO LONGER PRAY—
    NOW I DRINK DARK CHOCOLATE
        AND LET THE MOON SING TO ME.

Where to begin about the wonders
within the dilating mystery of the heart?

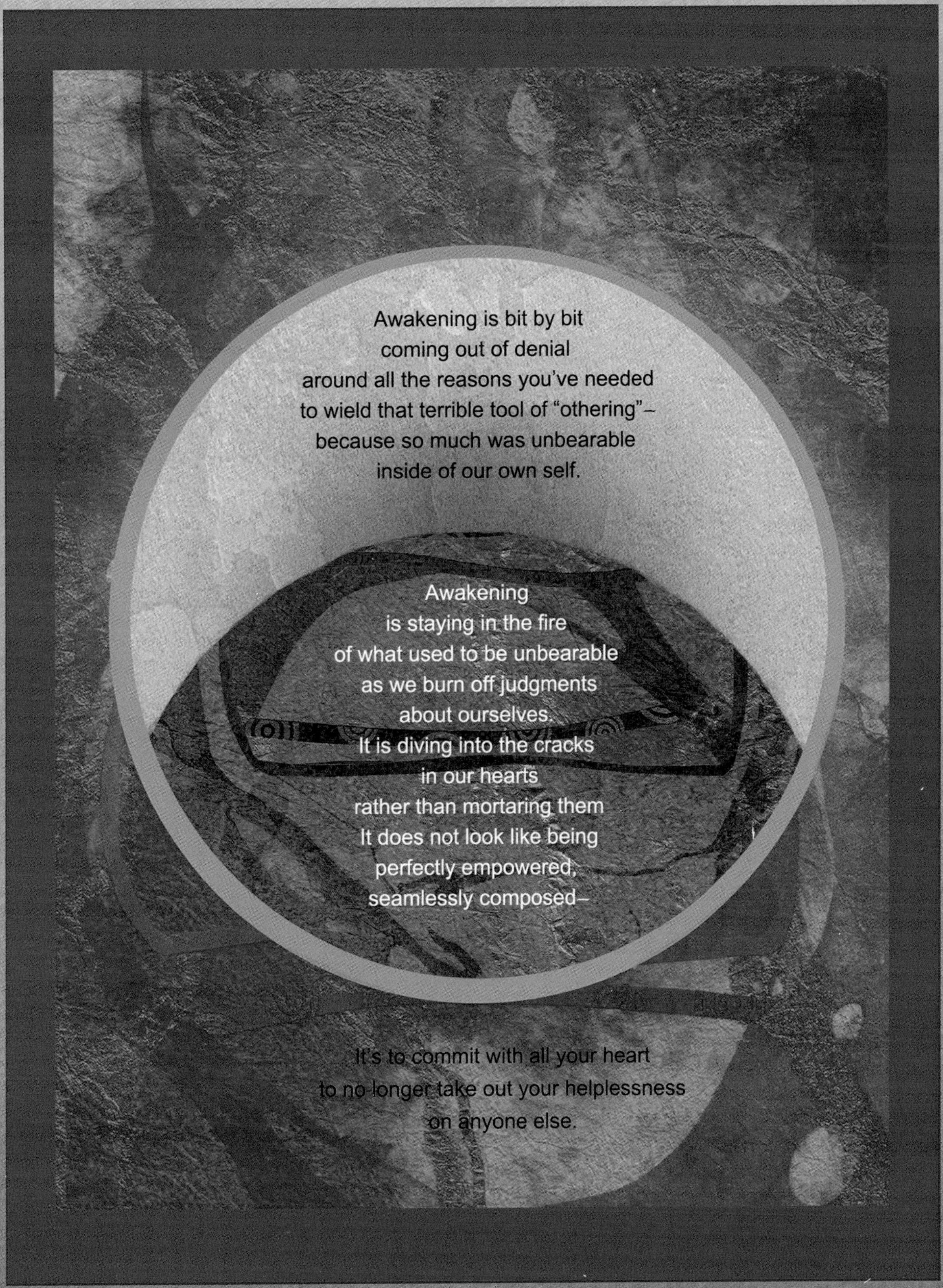

Awakening is bit by bit
coming out of denial
around all the reasons you've needed
to wield that terrible tool of "othering"–
because so much was unbearable
inside of our own self.

Awakening
is staying in the fire
of what used to be unbearable
as we burn off judgments
about ourselves.
It is diving into the cracks
in our hearts
rather than mortaring them
It does not look like being
perfectly empowered,
seamlessly composed–

It's to commit with all your heart
to no longer take out your helplessness
on anyone else.

Awakening is the at times compass-less
and often inglorious inner odyssey
toward the rough ruby
of all that is bruised
and true in the heart

The worst thing we ever did
was take the dance and the song out of prayer
made it sit up straight
and cross its legs

removed it of rejoicing
wiped clean its hip sway,
its questions,
its ecstatic yowl,
its tears.

I BECOME SANCTIFIED
WHEN MY FRAILTIES BLEED OUT
AND THERE'S NO BALM TO GRAB
SAVE THE SALVE OF HER VERSE
THAT DOESN'T SO MUCH CLOSE
THE WOUND AS GIVE PUR-
POSE TO ITS POURING.

sanctified

YES, BEFORE OUR POEMS BECOME CALLOUSED
WITH REVISION
LET THEM SHRIEK OFF THE PAGE OF SPONTANEITY

AND BEFORE OUR METAPHORS GET TOO REGULAR,
LET THE SUN STAY
A CONFLAGRATION OF HOMING PIGEONS
THAT FIGHTS THROUGH FIRE
EACH DAY TO FIND US.

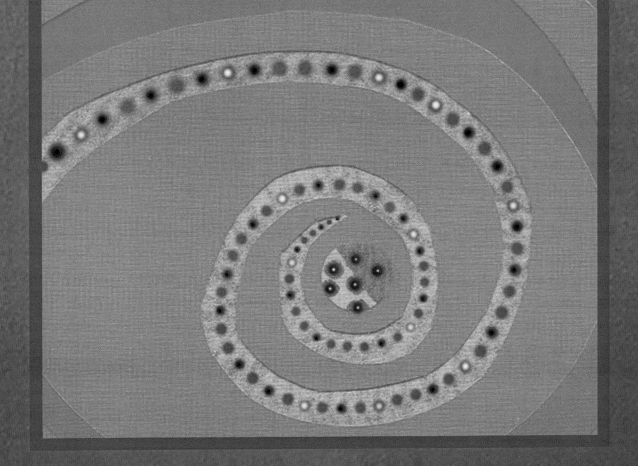

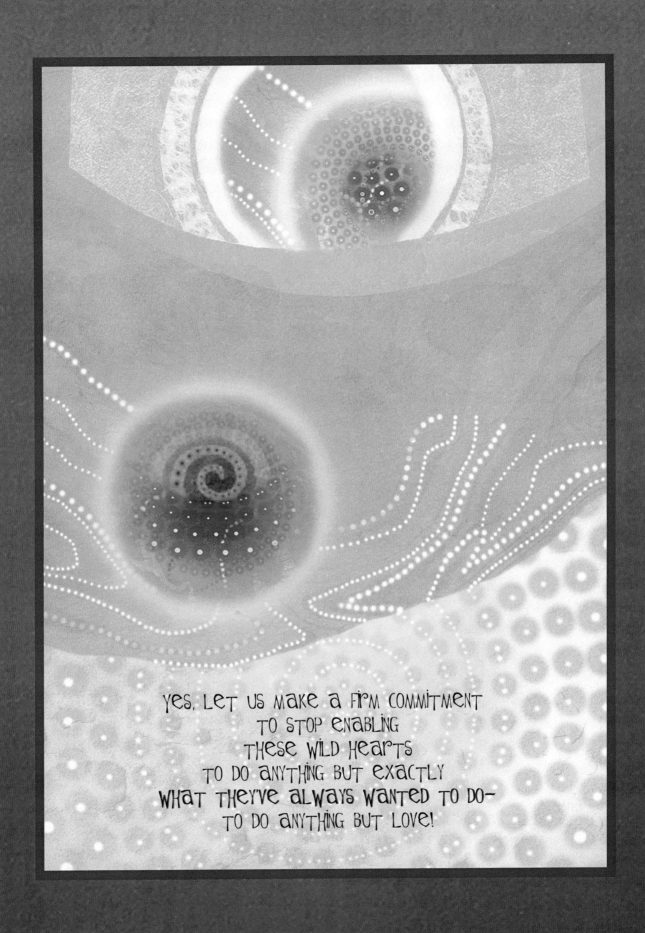

YES, LET US MAKE A FIRM COMMITMENT
TO STOP ENABLING
THESE WILD HEARTS
TO DO ANYTHING BUT EXACTLY
WHAT THEY'VE ALWAYS WANTED TO DO—
TO DO ANYTHING BUT LOVE!

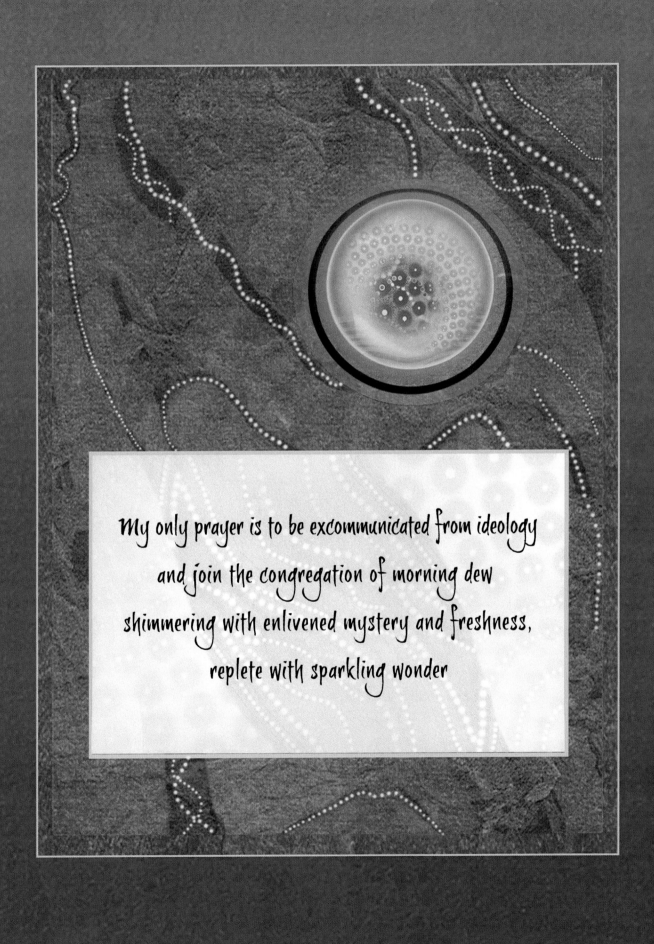

My only prayer is to be excommunicated from ideology
and join the congregation of morning dew
shimmering with enlivened mystery and freshness,
replete with sparkling wonder

I no longer pray—
        I go to the river
    and howl my ancient pain
        into the current.

I asked Hafiz for help with my poetry.
He said, "All poems already are,
like luminous birds in the spirit realm.
You simply must summon them."

Can you
believe it

that
we should be
fortunate enough
for beauty to
exist at
all?

I move like the moon.

Sometimes I am unavailable to give
my light and need to stay cloaked
in the necessary recovery
of my darkness.

Often I pray to Táhirih,
a great Persian poet and feminist
of the 1800's who would remove
her veil when addressing men
and was martyred
for speaking the irrepressible truth
in her heart
at age 38.
Her final words were,
"You can kill me as soon as you like,
but you will never stop
the emancipation of women."

HOBNOB WITH ALL THE GREAT DEAD POETS,
THINKERS, LOVERS,
ARTISTS, LEADERS OF TRUTH.

THEY STILL WANT A PLACE
TO POUR THEIR WONDER INTO THE WORLD
AND YOU ARE A GREAT VESSEL.

Suffering exists

to jostle you
awake,
to convince you
to shake
every illusion

that has clung to your soul

leeching your vastness

The tectonic plates
of the status quo
are meant to rumble,
Structures that could never hold you
are meant to
collapse—

their downfall is the revelation
of more of your totality.

more of your totality...

Security and stability
are not the ultimate foundations—
love is
and She is a wild, thrashing thing
and in Her desire for all of you
She will undo you from everything.

Who
would take the care
to create the delicate origami
of wildflower?

WHETHER OR NOT YOU TASTE THE SKY
YOU ARE BUILDING THE FUTURE
OF HUMANITY'S WINGS.

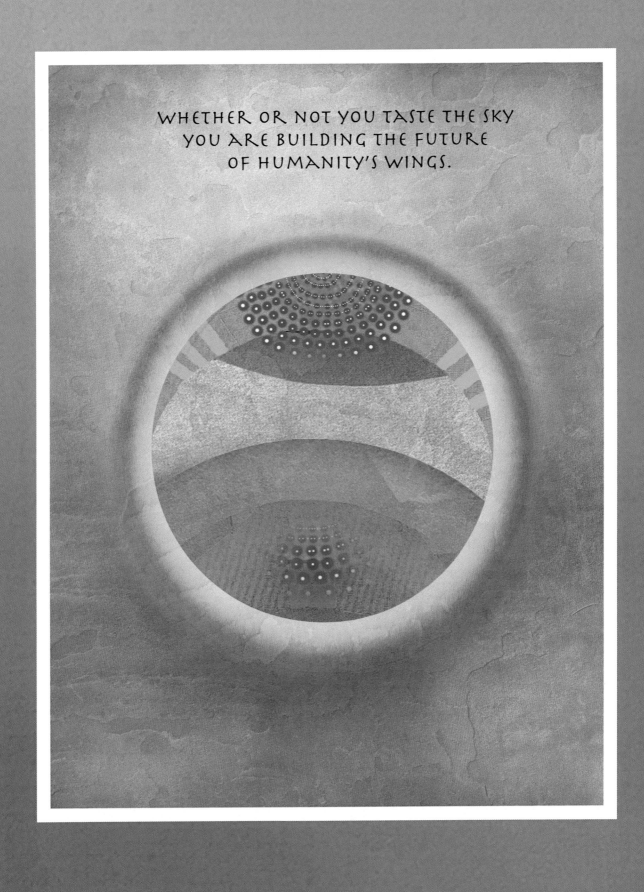

It's time to reframe and reclaim the phrase,
"I am too much"...

It's time to practice being okay
with it lathering ourselves
in it and basking in all
that we are—
      Here goes:

I'm too much!
I want to devour suns
for breakfast and kiss the center
     of every heart.

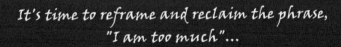

Let your too muchness
be your devotion—
God, after all,
is the Queen
of Too Much,
polyamorous
with every religion
and every heart as She
is and She does not stop
making her point after only one
galaxy.

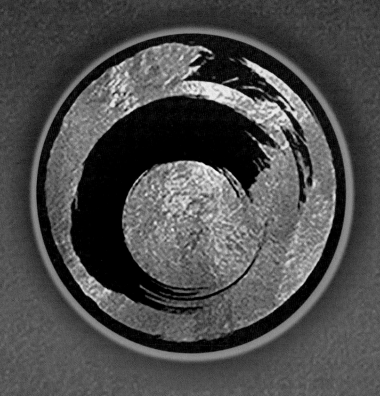

A poem
is where the flint of soul
strikes the stone of trauma
and makes a
spark.

IF MOTHERS RULED THE WORLD
THIS WORLD WOULD GO
FROM BARREN TO FERTILE,
FROM WASTELAND
TO ROSE GARDEN,
FROM REVENUE
TO RELATIONSHIP,
FROM BURNED OUT
TO POWERFUL, FULL BELLIED FLAME
ALMOST OVERNIGHT

I'M IN THE MOOD TO BE HIDEOUS.

TO UNQUALIFY

THE DARKNESS WITHIN ME

BY CEASING TO TALK OF LIGHT

TO ERASE SILVER LININGS.

I'M IN THE MOOD

TO COVER MYSELF WITH MUD

AND STOP TALKING ABOUT HOPE.

TO STOP RESCUING MYSELF

FROM MY DESPAIR

AND STOP REFRAMING MY DARKEST HOUR

WITH THE PEP TALK OF DAWN

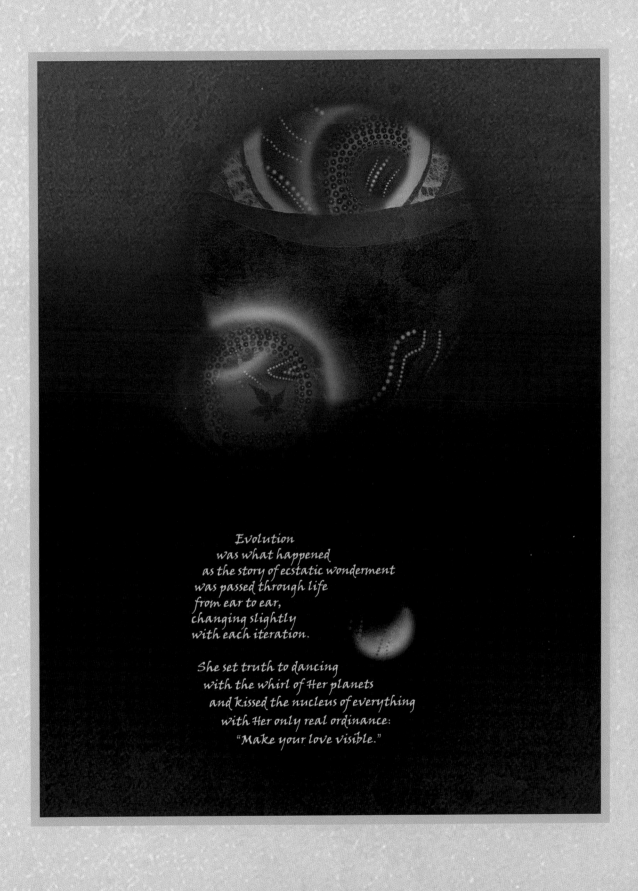

Evolution
  was what happened
    as the story of ecstatic wonderment
  was passed through life
  from ear to ear,
  changing slightly
  with each iteration.

  She set truth to dancing
    with the whirl of Her planets
      and kissed the nucleus of everything
    with Her only real ordinance:
      "Make your love visible."

Photo of Chelan by Shelly Peterson

Inspired poetry has been flowing through Chelan for years though her publishing journey is only a year and a half old. Her launch into sharing her poetry with the world has been mystical, transformational and filled with prayer experiments gone right. She is thrilled to now be offering speaking events nationally and internationally. Chelan is 33 years old and lives in a geographically spectacular region of Washington State in the US with her husband, Noah, and their two small, beautiful children, Amari and Nahanni. In her poetry and in her life, Chelan continually invites the fumbling, suffering parts of our human nature along with our divinity to meet for tea in the heart, to have a great laugh, celebrate our sacred grief and share a big hug. Along with *Taste the Sky*, she has authored two other books of poetry, *Susceptible to Light* and *Let Us Dance!: The Stumble and Whirl with The Beloved*. More to come soon!

www.chelanharkin.com

Photo of Rashani by Marie Claire Schultheis

A social activist and prolific artist since childhood, Rashani continues to be a resilient voice in the emerging inter-spiritual movement. Her non-sectarian offerings are rooted in nature, social justice, self-inquiry, the Deep Feminine, Wu-wei, ancient perennial wisdom traditions and several contemporary psycho-spiritual teachings. She has recorded 15 albums of Soetry (songs and poetry), published 40 books and has created more than 350 greeting cards in celebration of the diversity of timeless wisdom. A mother, lover, song gatherer, grief whisperer, builder & architect, tree planter, devoted gardener & landscape artist, Rashani has co-created two eco-sanctuaries on the Big Island of Hawaiʻi, where she currently resides. She has been facilitating retreats and offering councils, kirtans and participatory concerts throughout the world for the past 35 years and offers 2 and 4-week retreats at Kipukamaluhia Sanctuary—her home—in Hawaiʻi.

www.rashani.com

Other Books by Rashani include:

go slowly, breathe and smile, co-authored with Thich Nhat Hanh
Beyond Brokenness. (The Danish version is called *Sangen I Sorgen*)
The Time of Transformation is Here
Chakra Poems
A Soft Imminence of Rain: Celtic Poems by Alice O. Howell
A Cry of Windbells
My Bird Has Come Home
The Unfurling of an Artist: Early Collages and Calligraphy of Rashani Réa
Welcome to the Feast: In Celebration of Wholeness
Is The Bowl Empty or Is It Filled with Moonlight?: Turning Words and Bodhi Leaves
Mahalo: Visual Koans for the Pathless Journey
Always Choose Love
Moonlight on a Night Moth's Wing: A Fusion of Image and Word
True Golden Sand
Timeless Offerings
The Way Moonlight Touches
Shimmering Birthless: A Confluence of Verse and Image
An Unfolding of Love
Touched by Grace: Through a Temenos of Women
Territory of Wonder
Gossamer Mirrors
In Praise of Love: A Dialogue Between a Dove and a Ladybug
The Disappearance
The Threshold Between Loss and Revelation
A Brief Collision with Clockocracy
I Can Hear Her Breathing
Collaborating with the Inevitable
The Fire of Darkness: What Burned Me Away Completely, I Became
Only One Surrender
Nondual Reflections
Three Children's Stories, which include: *Present Moment, Colorful Moment: Sharing Present Moment Awareness with Children, Tao and the Moon* and *Can You Draw a Shooting Star?: A Child's Experience and Expression of Loss*
The Mercurial Impermanence of Aliveness
Who or What Remains?
Pencil Sharpeners and Thunderstorms
A Coven of Dakinis: In Honor of Thirteen Women Who Have Touched My Life
Waves into Water
nameless: a riff of 44 images complemented by poetry

....

Other Books by Chelan include:

Susceptible to Light: Poetry by Chelan Harkin
Let Us Dance!: The Stumble and Whirl with the Beloved
Wild Grace (to be published in the Fall of 2022)